THE POWER OF THE MIND

"Thou wilt keep him in perfect peace, whose mind is stayed on thee: because he trusteth in thee."

Isaiah 26:3

By
Franklin N. Abazie

The Power of the Mind

COPYRIGHT 2018 BY Franklin N Abazie
ISBN: 978-1-945-133-32-9

All right reserved. This book or any portion thereof may not be reproduced or used in any manner whatsoever without the express written permission of the publisher, except for the use of brief quotations in a book review. All Bible quotes are from King James Version and others as noted.

Published by: F N ABAZIE PUBLISHING HOUSE---
a.k.a,
Empowerment Bookstore:

That I may publish with the voice of thanksgiving and tell of all thy wondrous works. **Psalms26:7**

To order additional copies, wholesales or booking: Call the Church office (973-372-7518)
or Empowerment Bookstore Hotline 973-393-8518
Worship address:
343 Sanford Avenue Newark New Jersey 07106
Administrative Head Office address:
33 Schley Street Newark New Jersey 07112
Email:pastorfranknto@yahoo.com
Website www.fnabaziehealingministries.org
Publishing House: www.fnabaziepublishinghouse.org

This book is a production of F N Abazie Publishing House.

A publication Arms of Miracle of God Ministries 2018
First Edition

CONTENTS

THE MANDATE OF THE COMMISSION..............iv

ARMS OF THE COMMISSION...............................v

INTRODUCTION..viii

CHAPTER 1

1. The Mystery of the Mind 29

CHAPTER 2

2. The Mind of Christ..42

CHAPTER 3

3. Prayer of Salvation..63

CHAPTER 4

4. About the Author...73

THE MANDATE OF THE COMMISSION

"THE MOMENT IS DUE TO IMPACT YOUR WORLD THROUGH THE REVIVAL OF THE HEALING & MIRACLE MINISTRY OF JESUS CHRIST OF NAZARETH.

I AM SENDING YOU TO RESTORE HEALTH UNTO THEE AND I WILL HEAL THEE OF THY WOUNDS, SAID THE LORD OF HOST."

ARMS OF THE COMMISSION

1) F N Abazie Ministries-Miracle of God Ministries (Miracle Chapel Intl)

2) F N Abazie TV Ministries: Global Television Ministry Outreach.

3) F N Abazie Radio Ministries: Radio Broadcasting Outreach.

4) F N Abazie Publishing House: Book Publication.

5) F N Abazie Bible School: also called Word of Healing Bible School (W.O.H.B.S)

6) F N Abazie Evangelistic Ass: Miracle of God Ministries: Global Crusade

7) Empowerment Bookstore: Book distribution.

8) F N Abazie Helping Hands: Meeting the help of the needy world wide

9) F N Abazie Disaster Recovery Mission: Global Disaster Recovery.

10) F N Abazie Prison Ministry: Prison Ministry for all convicts "Second chance"

Some of our ministry arms are waiting the appointed time to commence

INTRODUCTION

"Keep thy heart with all diligence; for out of it are the issues of life..." **Proverb4:23**

I may never get the chance to meet you in person, but I am very glad to say hello to you right here. I love the power of literature. I come to you through this small book to talk about the power of the mind.

One man said that there is a great dichotomy between the brain and the mind but I just want to talk a bit of the mind from the Holy Scriptures.

The two obvious battles engaging the mind are neurosis - When someone is in their right mind but dealing with internal conflict of the mind. (outside you look okay to others, but inside of you, you have almost lost your right mind). The second kind of battle is called psychosis when someone has lost touch with reality. Often the society labels them insane. we must always guide our mind jealously.

I love that fact that you are reading this small book. In deed this book is designed to help your spirit man.

Over my few years in the gospel ministry, I have notice that our only challenge is the daily conflict that goes on in our minds.

It is written *"And be renewed in the spirit of your mind."* **Ephesians4:23**

"And be not conformed to this world: but be ye transformed by the renewing of your mind, that ye may prove what is that good, and acceptable, and perfect, will of God." **Romans12:2.**

Hopefully this small book will make sense to you. May the Holy Spirit help us in Jesus Name., Come with me..!

Happy Reading!

"God want us to train our mind and be focus on the things that matter most to us in life."

Franklin N Abazie

"If you cannot see far through the power of the mind, you will never go far in life."

Franklin N Abazie

"For who hath known the mind of the Lord, that he may instruct him? but we have the mind of Christ."

1cor2:16

"Let this mind be in you, which was also in Christ Jesus:"
Phil2:5

"And be renewed in the spirit of your mind;"
Ephesians 4:23

"And be not conformed to this world: but be ye transformed by the renewing of your mind, that ye may prove what is that good, and acceptable, and perfect, will of God."
Romans12:2

"For out of the heart proceed evil thoughts, murders, adulteries, fornications, thefts, false witness, blasphemies"
Mathew 15:19

"Thou wilt keep him in perfect peace, whose mind is stayed on thee: because he trusteth in thee."
Isaiah26:3

"Finally, brothers and sisters, whatever is true, whatever is noble, whatever is right, whatever is pure, whatever is lovely, whatever is admirable—if anything is excellent or praiseworthy—think about such things."

Philippians 4:8

Wise quote

Our behavior is higher and greater than knowledge, because in life there are many situations where knowledge will fail you, but you good behavior, integrity, and honesty will always sail us through.

Although without a two way communication, there is no relationship; I say also without respect there is no love. Listen to me, without trust, there is no reason to continue the relationship.

Always treat people the way you want to be treated. Remember to talk to people the way you want them to talk back to you.

In life respect is always earned not given. Difficulties in our life do not come to destroy our lives, but rather to manifest our hidden potentials and power. As winners, we must confront and conquer every challenge in life.

Remember….. Without challenges in our life, we wouldn't be who we are today. Be grateful for the good and the bad. When someone does something wrong, don't forget all the things they did right. Honesty is very expensive gift, do not expect it from cheap people

FAVOR CONFESSION

Father thank you for making me righteous and accepted through the blood of Jesus Christ. Because of that, I am blessed and highly favored by God. I am the subject of your affection. Your favor surrounds me as a shield, and the first thing that people see around me is your favored shield.

Thank you that I have favor with you and man today. All day long people go out of their way to bless me and help me. I have favor with everyone that I deal with today. Doors that were once closed are now opened for me. I receive preferential treatment, and I have special privileges, I am Gods favored child.

No good thing will he withhold from me. Because of Gods favor my enemies cannot triumph over my life. I have supernatural increase and promotion. I declare restoration to everything that the devil has stolen from my life. I have honor in the midst of my adversaries and an increase in assets, especially in real estate and expansion of territories.

Because I am highly favored by God, I experience great victories, supernatural turnarounds, and miraculous breakthrough in the midst of great impossibilities. I receive recognition, prominence, and honor. Petitions are granted to me even by ungodly authorities. Policies, rules, regulations, and laws are changed and reverse on my behalf.

I win battles that I don't even have to fight, because God fights them for me. This is the day, the set time and the designated moment for me to experience the free favor of God, that profusely and lavishly abound on my behalf in Jesus name. Amen.

HIS DESTINY WAS THE CROSS….

HIS PURPOSE WAS LOVE…..

HIS REASON WAS YOU….

"And be not conformed to this world: but be ye transformed by the renewing of your mind, that ye may prove what is that good, and acceptable, and perfect, will of God."

Romans12:2

Prayer points

"If ye shall ask any thing in my name, I will do it.."
John14:14

Holy Spirit of God frustrate and disappoint, every one that is against my life and family, in the name of Jesus.

Father Lord destroy every demonic networks and traps against my progress in life in the name of Jesus.

Fire of God, destroy every demonic projection and curses against my life and destiny in the name of Jesus.

Every spell and curses pronounced against my destiny, break, in the name of Jesus.

Hand of God cage every power militating against my rising in life, in the name of Jesus.

Power of God silent every voice raising a counter motion against my elevation, in the mighty name of Jesus.

Blood of Jesus neutralize every spirit of Balaam hired to hinder my life, ministry, and career, the name of Jesus.

Fire of God destroy every curse that I have brought into my life through ignorance and disobedience, break by fire, in the name of Jesus.

Ancient of day destroy every power harassing my ministry in the name of Jesus.

Father God deliver me from invincible forces militating against my life and destiny.

Power of God frustrate every coven and demonic network, designed to frustrate and hinder my success in life, in the name of Jesus.

I dismantle every strong hold designed to imprison my talent in the mighty name of Jesus.

I reject every cycle of frustration, in the name of Jesus.

Power of God paralyze every agent assigned to frustrate my life in the name of Jesus.

Finger of God, grant me supernatural speed against all my contenders in the name of Jesus.

By the blood of Jesus, I destroy every familiar spirit caging my life and career.

Fire of God arrest every demonic agents, assigned to police my destiny and marriage.

By the blood of Jesus, I proclaim no weapon fashioned against me shall ever prosper.

Holy Spirit of God break me through and forward in life in the mighty name of Jesus.

God, smash me and renew my strength, in the name of Jesus.

Holy Spirit, open my eyes to see beyond the visible to the invisible, in the name of Jesus.

Father Lord grant me strength and power in the name of Jesus

O Lord, liberate my spirit to follow the leading of the Holy Spirit.

Holy Spirit, teach me to pray through problems instead of praying about, it in the name of Jesus.

Father Lord, deliver me from the false accusation in life, in the name of Jesus

By the blood of Jesus, every evil spiritual padlock and evil chain hindering my success, be roasted, in the name of Jesus.

By the blood of Jesus I rebuke every spirit of spiritual deafness and blindness in my life, in the name of Jesus.

Father Lord, empower me to dominate the enemy of my destiny in the name of Jesus.

Jesus Christ of Nazareth, heal my infirmities in the name of Jesus

Lord, anoint my eyes and my ears that they may see and hear wonderous things from heaven.

Father Lord, anoint me with power and authority to dominate all my enemies in the name of Jesus.

Fire of God roast every giant rising up against my life and career.

Holy Spirit of God destroy all my oppressors in the name of Jesus.

Angels of good new, bring my good news to me in the mighty name of Jesus.

Every strong man holding me down, lose your hold now in the name of Jesus.

I nullify every demonic prediction over my life in the name of Jesus.

By the blood of Jesus, I flush out every polluted deposit of the enemy in my life.

By the blood of Jesus, I paralyze every enemy of my promotion in the name of Jesus.

Holy Ghost fire, ignite the fire of revival in my life.

By the blood of Jesus, I declare victory over every conflicting trial.

By the Blood of Jesus, I command the arrest of every demonic spirit, militating against my life

By the blood of Jesus, I proclaimed the blood of Jesus, over every device of the enemy.

By the blood of Jesus, I revoke stagnation and hardship over my life in the name of Jesus.

Holy Ghost fire, destroy every satanic arrangement in my life, in the name of Jesus.
Every witchcraft utterance and projections, made against me, be overthrown, in the name of Jesus.

O God, make my enemies like a wheel as the stubble before the wind, in the name of Jesus.

I reverse the effect of every witchcraft summoning of my spirit, in the name of Jesus.

O Lord, persecute my enemies with thy tempest and make them afraid with thy storm, in the Name of Jesus.

Every witchcraft identification mark, be wiped off by the blood of Jesus.

O Lord, let my enemies be confounded and troubled, in the name of Jesus.

I frustrate every witchcraft exchange of my virtues, in the name of Jesus.

All the assembly of the violent men be scattered, in the name of Jesus.

Anything planted in my life by witchcraft, come out now, in the name of Jesus.

O Lord, break down the hedges of the wicked and bring their strongholds to run, in the name of Jesus.

Every witchcraft seed in my life be roasted, in the name of Jesus.

I shall not be afraid for the terror by night, or for the arrow that flieth by day, in the name of Jesus.

Let each step taken by witchcraft against me lead them to greater destructions, in the name of Jesus.

Thousand shall fall at my side and ten thousand at my right hand, but it shall not come near me, in the name of Jesus.

I declare my environment not-flying zone for witchcraft birds, in the name of Jesus.

Mines eyes shall see my desires on my enemies, in the name of Jesus.

I cut off the roots of witchcraft in the water, in the name of Jesus.

Thou power that troubled the Egyptians, trouble my enemies, in the name of Jesus.

Anything deposited in my life by marine witchcraft, come out now, in the name of Jesus.

O gate of brass and bars of iron, working against me, be broken, in the name of Jesus.
Anything deposited in my life by household witchcraft, come out now, in the name of Jesus.

The wicked shall be grieved and his desired shall perish, in the name of Jesus.

Let the rivers of my enemies be turned into wilderness, in the name of Jesus.

I come against every form of barrenness in my life, in the name of Jesus.

Through God, I shall do valiantly, for it is He that shall tread down my enemies, in the name of Jesus.

Let all those who consult darkness against me be disgraced, in the name of Jesus.

O Lord, set a wicked man over the wicked, in the name of Jesus.

The Lord is on my side, I will not fear what man can do unto me, in the name of Jesus.

Let the days of my enemies be cut off and let another take his office, in the name of Jesus.

Depart from me, ye evil doers, for I will keep the commandments of my God, in the Name of Jesus.

As the enemy loved cursing, let it come unto him, in the name of Jesus.

Lord, deliver me from the oppression of man, in the name of Jesus.

As the enemy delighted not in blessing, so let it be far from him, in the name of Jesus.

As the enemy clothed him with cursing, like as a garment, so let it come into his bowel like water and like oil into his bones, in the name of Jesus.

O thou that troubleth the Israel of Mountain of fire and Miracle ministries, the God of Elijah shall trouble you today.

O God, arise and uproot anything you did not plant inside the Mountain of Fire and Miracle Ministries, in the name of Jesus.

Every enemy of the Mountain of Fire and Miracle Ministries, scatter, in the name of Jesus.

Let the fire of revival fall upon Mountain of Fire and Miracle Ministries, in the name of Jesus.

CHAPTER 1
The Mystery of the Mind

"And be renewed in the spirit of your mind." **Ephesians 4:23**

"Thou wilt keep him in perfect peace, whose mind is stayed on thee: because he trusteth in thee." **Isaiah 26:3**

The mind is the decision maker, the factory for knowledge, the warehouse, and memory bank of human-beings, capable to retain, to store, and memorize events and remember experience in life.

One of the unsolved mystery in ages, is the networking between the mind and the brain. Our mind is indeed a smart working computer. Our mind can be program positively and negatively. Our mind can be program for success and for failure.

It is written *"For as he thinketh in his heart, so is he: Eat and drink, saith he to thee; but his heart is not with thee."* **Proverb 23:7**

Generally, our mind has the following conscience;

Pure Conscience

"Unto the pure all things are pure: but unto them that are defiled and unbelieving is nothing pure; but even their mind and conscience is defiled." **Titus1:15**

Dead Conscience

"How much more shall the blood of Christ, who through the eternal Spirit offered himself without spot to God, purge your conscience from dead works to serve the living God?" **Hebrew9:14**

Evil Conscience

"Speaking lies in hypocrisy; having their conscience seared with a hot iron;" **1timothy4:2**

Good Conscience

"And Paul, earnestly beholding the council, said, Men and brethren, I have lived in all good conscience before God until this day." **Acts23:1**

Chapter 1 - The Mystery of the Mind

"And herein do I exercise myself, to have always a conscience void to offence toward God, and toward men." **Acts24:16**

One man said, "If you fail to plan, you have planned to fail in life." The mind is the place where we make daily decisions. Any time we suffer any attack in the mind people tend to label us mentally sick, or insane. We must therefore protect, and guide our mind from every wiles and schemes of the devil.

It is written *"Keep thy heart with all diligence; for out of it are the issues of life."* **Proverb4:23**

As believers our mind must be constantly renewed in the word of God. We must form the habit of reading and meditating in the Holy Scripture daily.

One man said, *"Whenever you are depressed, you are living in the past. Whenever you are anxious, you are living in the future. But when you are at peace, you are living in the present."*

It is written, *"Keep thy heart with all diligence; for out of it are the issues of life."* **Proverb4:23**

"And be renewed in the spirit of your mind." **Ephesians4:23**

If you are determined to setup your mind towards a realistic goal. No devil on earth can stop you from achieving it. The greatness of any man is his/her ability to decide in their heart.

"For as he thinketh in his heart, so is he: Eat and drink, saith he to thee; but his heart is not with thee." **Proverb23:7**

"But the natural man receiveth not the things of the Spirit of God: for they are foolishness unto him: neither can he know them, because they are spiritually discerned." **1cor2:14**

Chapter 1 - The Mystery of the Mind

The above scripture is an instruction for us to always be in the spirit. If you are in the Spirit, you will hear the voice of God. Apostle John was in the Spirit on the lord's day and he heard the great voice of God..
I was in the Spirit on the Lord's day, and heard behind me a great voice, as of a trumpet.

To be in the Spirit is to be in tune. To be in the Spirit is to be on time, at the right place at the right time. Although Apostle Paul admonished us to think of great things in life, the primary assignment of the devil is to blind our minds as believers.

"In whom the god of this world hath blinded the minds of them which believe not, lest the light of the glorious gospel of Christ, who is the image of God, should shine unto them." **2cor4:4**

"The heart is deceitful above all things, and desperately sick; who can understand it?" **Jer17:9.**

"Finally, brethren, whatsoever things are true, whatsoever things are honest, whatsoever things are just, whatsoever things are pure, whatsoever things are lovely, whatsoever things are of good report; if there be any virtue, and if there be any praise, think on these things."

The Mind is the birthplace of decisions in life

"And if it seem evil unto you to serve the Lord, choose you this day whom ye will serve; whether the gods which your fathers served that were on the other side of the flood, or the gods of the Amorites, in whose land ye dwell: but as for me and my house, we will serve the Lord." **Joshua 24:16**

"I call heaven and earth to record this day against you, that I have set before you life and death, blessing and cursing: therefore choose life, that both thou and thy seed may live:" **Deut 30:19**

I have heard a number of miserable stories, people who made a detrimental decision that negatively affected their lives forever.

Chapter 1 - The Mystery of the Mind

It is written, *"For God hath not given us the spirit of fear; but of power, and of love, and of a sound mind."* **2timothy1:7**

For any man or woman to have a sound mind, they must be in constant communication with Father God in prayer.

It is written *"For ye have not received the spirit of bondage again to fear; but ye have received the Spirit of adoption, whereby we cry, Abba, Father."* **Romans8:15**

"A journey of a thousand miles begins with a single step."—**Lao Tzu**

To make up our mind and decide, is the first step into anything great in life. Although we can be influenced by mentors, siblings, parents, and prevailing environmental pressure. Every man must examine their circumstances uniquely. We must take into account our emotions, and psychological state so that we can cope with prevailing challenges.

"And be renewed in the spirit of your mind;" **Ephesians 4:23**

"Keep thy heart with all diligence; for out of it are the issues of life." **Proverb 4:23**

"For who hath known the mind of the Lord, that he may instruct him? but we have the mind of Christ." **1cor 2:16**

"Let this mind be in you, which was also in Christ Jesus:" **Phil 2:5**

For anyone to accomplish great things in life or becoming a failure in life is a function of our mind set. Soldiers think differently especially in the battle filed.

Your thoughts affect what happens to you.

We are a product of decision. Our thought affects what happens to our life. Our mind will take a thought and turn it into an experience. Whatever you say in the mind, has power to affect how you feel. Our thoughts are directly related to experience in life.

Chapter 1 - The Mystery of the Mind

Likewise also, positive thought attracts positive things to happen to us. For as he thinketh in his heart, so is he: Eat and drink, saith he to thee; but his heart is not with thee.

Whatever we focus on we can attract in life

Whatever you focus your mind on, you will eventually attract in life. *"And the Lord said, Behold, the people is one, and they have all one language; and this they begin to do: and now nothing will be restrained from them, which they have imagined to do."* **Genesis11:6.**

The mind can be trained to be focused. Whenever we concentrate our mind on one thing, we do well in life.

David said *"One thing have I desired of the Lord, that will I seek after; that I may dwell in the house of the Lord all the days of my life, to behold the beauty of the Lord, and to enquire in his temple."* **Psalms27:4**

Apostle Paul put it this way

"Brethren, I count not myself to have apprehended: but this one thing I do, forgetting those things which are behind, and reaching forth unto those things which are before, I press toward the mark for the prize of the high calling of God in Christ Jesus." **Phil3:13-14**

For our greatness to emerge in our life time, we must be focus on one thing. I admonish you to train your mind to be focus on one thing and you watch and see what God will do with your life.

There is no poor man, we only have poor mindset

The bible says *"The rich and poor meet together: the Lord is the maker of them all."* **Proverb22:2**

"For the poor shall never cease out of the land: therefore I command thee, saying, Thou shalt open thine hand wide unto thy brother, to thy poor, and to thy needy, in thy land." **Deut15:11**

Chapter 1 - The Mystery of the Mind

The truth is that both the rich and the poor do not think alike. The rich always want to exact and rule over the poor man. And the poor man- I mean the borrower is a servant in his life time

"The rich ruleth over the poor, and the borrower is servant to the lender."
Prover22:7.

Although the rich mind acquires assets, the poor mind only thinks of luck. The smart man thinks of cause and effect, but the poor mind acquires liabilities involuntarily. We are not born poor, we only think poor thoughts. If you think rich, you will be rich in life.

Often the rich mind thinks, prepare, and plan before taking financial actions in life, but the poor mind is in a haste, reckless in making a financial decision. The rich mind thinks of assets and investment.But the poor man thinks liabilities and expenses.

The Power of excellence

Unless you walk with the Holy Spirit, you will never do great things in life. It takes the Holy Spirit to develop an excellent Spirit. *"Then this Daniel was preferred above the presidents and princes, because an excellent spirit was in him; and the king thought to set him over the whole realm."* **Daniel 6:3**

Overcoming Fear

It takes boldness and a sound mind to overcome fear in life. It is written There were they in great fear, where no fear was: for God hath scattered the bones of him that encampeth against thee: thou hast put them to shame, because God hath despised them.

Power of Desire

We must always believe that we will get what we desire in life. It is written "Therefore I say unto you, What things soever ye desire, when ye pray, believe that ye receive them, and ye shall have them."

Chapter 2 - The Mind of Christ

Power of Imagination

If you can imagine a great future in a picture or say mental image, God will make it happen in our life. And the Lord said, Behold, the people is one, and they have all one language; and this they begin to do: and now nothing will be restrained from them, which they have imagined to do.

The mind is a terrible thing to waste. Invest in knowledge. Invest in mentorship. Go and learn a new trade, a new vocation. Look for training centers and be counted among those who are rebuilding the society.

We must keep our mind young by reading, mediating, and practicing righteousness, humility in life. We must owe no man nothing but love.

It is written *"Owe no man any thing, but to love one another: for he that loveth another hath fulfilled the law."* **Romans13:8**

"Jesus said unto him, Thou shalt love the Lord thy God with all thy heart, and with all thy soul, and with all thy mind." **Mathew22:37**

CHAPTER 2
The Mind of Christ

"For who hath known the mind of the Lord, that he may instruct him? but we have the mind of Christ." **1cor2:16**

Our mind must be renewed daily if we must have the mind of Christ. It is written *"And be not conformed to this world: but be ye transformed by the renewing of your mind, that ye may prove what is that good, and acceptable, and perfect, will of God."* **Romans12:2**

Most people keep thinking the same kind of thoughts, and visualize the same mental images in an unconscious involuntary motion.

What is the mind of Christ?

The opening scripture said, *"'For who has known the mind of the Lord that he may instruct him?' But we have the mind of Christ."* **1cor2:16**

The mind of Christ is the mind of love. The mind of love is a giving spirit. We are told *"For God so loved the world, that he gave his only begotten Son, that whosoever believeth in him should not perish, but have everlasting life."* **John3:16**

Jesus said *"Draw nigh to God, and he will draw nigh to you. Cleanse your hands, ye sinners; and purify your hearts, ye double minded."*

Humility and meekness must become our primary reason for living. We must become humble, with a giving and loving heart. A heart for God is a heart for the people of God.

God said *"And we have known and believed the love that God hath to us. God is love; and he that dwelleth in love dwelleth in God, and God in him."* **1John4:16**

Talking about Jesus, the word of God said *"Let this mind be in you, which was also in Christ Jesus:"*

Chapter 2 - The Mind of Christ

"Who, being in the form of God, thought it not robbery to be equal with God:"

"But made himself of no reputation, and took upon him the form of a servant, and was made in the likeness of men:"

"And being found in fashion as a man, he humbled himself, and became obedient unto death, even the death of the cross."
Phil 2:5-8

Every believers should have the mind of Christ. The mind of Christ is a thirst to seek the face of God in prayer, a mind of Christ is a hunger to see souls saved in the kingdom of God. By this I mean, a desire, to see sinners come to Christ. (Salvation for all)

"For the Son of man is come to seek and to save that which was lost.."
Luke19:10

Our approach to life and attitude should reflect that of Christ Jesus: Who, being in the form of God, thought it not robbery to be equal with God.

"But made himself of no reputation, and took upon him the form of a servant, and was made in the likeness of men:"

And being found in fashion as a man, he humbled himself, and became obedient unto death, even the death of the cross. The mind of Christ is to develop a loving and compassionate heart.

"And when the Lord saw her, he had compassion on her, and said unto her, Weep not."

The mind of Christ is a heart of prayer. *"But Jesus often withdrew to lonely places and prayed."* The mind of Christ is the mind of the Holy Spirit. *"But God hath revealed them unto us by his Spirit: for the Spirit searcheth all things, yea, the deep things of God."*

"For what man knoweth the things of a man, save the spirit of man which is in him? even so the things of God knoweth no man, but the Spirit of God.

Chapter 2 - The Mind of Christ

Now we have received, not the spirit of the world, but the spirit which is of God; that we might know the things that are freely given to us of God." **1cor2:10-12**

Talking about the Holy Spirit Isaiah said…. *"And the spirit of the Lord shall rest upon him, the spirit of wisdom and understanding, the spirit of counsel and might, the spirit of knowledge and of the fear of the Lord; And shall make him of quick understanding in the fear of the Lord: and he shall not judge after the sight of his eyes, neither reprove after the hearing of his ears:"* **Isiah11:2-3**

The mind of Christ is a heart of faith. The mind of Christ is the mindset to succeed in life. The mind of Christ is boldness and authority to survive prevailing challenges and go through tough and difficult times. In this prevailing times, only those with the mind of Christ will make it big time.

"But the path of the just is as the shining light, that shineth more and more unto the perfect day." **Proverb4:18**

"This book of the law shall not depart out of thy mouth; but thou shalt meditate therein day and night, that thou mayest observe to do according to all that is written therein: for then thou shalt make thy way prosperous, and then thou shalt have good success." **Joshua1:8**

The mind of Christ is to live an overcomer life. It is written *"There hath no temptation taken you but such as is common to man: but God is faithful, who will not suffer you to be tempted above that ye are able; but will with the temptation also make a way to escape, that ye may be able to bear it."* **1cor10:13.**

"For whatsoever is born of God overcometh the world: and this is the victory that overcometh the world, even our faith." **1John5:4**

"Ye are of God, little children, and have overcome them: because greater is he that is in you, than he that is in the world." **1John4:4**

Chapter 2 - The Mind of Christ

"And he said unto them, Ye are from beneath; I am from above: ye are of this world; I am not of this world." **John8:23**

"And he answered, Fear not: for they that be with us are more than they that be with them." **2King6:16**

CONCLUSION

"And be not conformed to this world: but be ye transformed by the renewing of your mind, that ye may prove what is that good, and acceptable, and perfect, will of God." **Romans12:2**

Our mind is the memory bank of life experiences. Our mind is the factory and ware house of our life. We must jealously guide our heart, spirit soul and will with every diligent in our life.

"Therefore if any man be in Christ, he is a new creature: old things are passed away; behold, all things are become new. **2cor5:17**

"This book of the law shall not depart out of thy mouth; but thou shalt meditate therein day and night, that thou mayest observe to do according to all that is written therein: for then thou shalt make thy way prosperous, and then thou shalt have good success." **Joshua1:8**

The mind of Christ is to live an overcomers life. It is written *"There hath no temptation taken you but such as is common to man: but God is faithful, who will not suffer you to be tempted above that ye are able; but will with the temptation also make a way to escape, that ye may be able to bear it."* **1cor10:13.**

"For whatsoever is born of God overcometh the world: and this is the victory that overcometh the world, even our faith." **1John5:4**

"Ye are of God, little children, and have overcome them: because greater is he that is in you, than he that is in the world." **1John4:4**

Chapter 2 - The Mind of Christ

Now repeat this prayer after me;

Say Lord Jesus, I accept you today, as my Lord and my savior, forgive me of my sins wash me with your blood. Right now, I believe, I am sanctified, I am save, I am free, I am free from the Power of sin to serve the Lord Jesus. Thank you Lord for saving me. Amen.

Congratulations: YOU ARE NOW A BORN AGAIN CHRISTIAN

What must I do to determine my divine visitation?

To determine divine visitation you must be born again. The word says as many as received him, to them gave He power to become the sons of God. Even to them that believe on his name.

To qualify for divine visitation do the following sincerely

1) Acknowledge that you are a sinner and that He died for you. **Rom3:23**.

2) Repent of your sins. **Acts 3:19, Luke13:5, 2Peter3:9**

3) Believe in your heart that Jesus died for your sin. **Romans10:10**

4) Confess Jesus as the Lord over your life. **Romans10:10, Acts2:21**

Now repeat this Prayer after me

Say Lord Jesus, I accept you today, as my Lord and my savior, forgive me of my sins wash me with your blood. Right now, I believe, I am sanctified, I am save, I am free, I am free from the Power of sin to serve the Lord Jesus. Thank you Lord for saving me. Amen. Congratulations: YOU ARE NOW A BORN AGAIN CHRISTAIN

I adjure you to watch the Spirit of God bear witness with your Spirit confirming His word with signs following.

Chapter 2 - The Mind of Christ

The word says The Spirit itself beareth witness with our spirit, that we are the children of God. Join a bible believing church or join us on our weekly and Sunday worship services at 343 Sanford Avenue Newark New Jersey 07106.

WISDOM KEYS

Every Productive Society is a society heading to the top

Millions of Nigerians run away from Nigeria, very few Nigerians stay in Nigeria.

My decision to return Nigeria is the will of God for my life

My short coming in America after 18 years, trained me to be wise, to think, reflect and reason appropriately.

If you train your mind to reason it will train your hands to earn money.

It is absurd to use the money of the heathen to build the kingdom of the living God.

Every Ministry reveals its agenda and goal either at the beginning or at the end. Be careful of your life it is your first Ministry.

The average American mind is conditioned for a continual quest to get new things and (discard the former) and throw away old things.

Chapter 2 - The Mind of Christ

When I considered well, my BMW jeep became my initial deposit for the work of the ministry in Nigeria

Everyone is waiting for you to change your mind until you change your thinking nothing changes around you.

Multiple academic degrees in other discipline gave me the chance to think, reflect and reason

What so everyone are thinking and reflecting at the moment reveals you to the time and the now factor

All events and intents are the product of precise thought processes, accurate reason every event is designed for a designated timeline

Wisdom is your ability to think, to create and invent. If you can think wise enough you will come out of penury

The distance between you and success is your creative ability to think reason and reflect accurate.

Success is the result of hard work, commitment resolve and determination learning from past mistakes and failing.

If you organize your mind you have organized your life and destiny.

There is a thin line between success and failure. If you look above and beyond you are on your way to success.

Wealth is your ability to think, power is your ability to reason and success is your ability to be informed.

If you can make use of your mind by thinking and reasoning God will make use of your life and destiny.

Think and Be Great

Reflect, Reason, think and be great

Famous people are born of woman

Chapter 2 - The Mind of Christ

That you will make it is your intention; that you will survive is your resolve, that you will succeed with changes is your determination, personal efforts and hard work.

No man was born a failure. Lack of vision is the end product of failure.

Working with mental patients encourages and aspire me to be a productive observant and dedicated to my assignment.

Successful people are not magicians, it is the will power combined with hard work, and determination and a resolve to succeed that make them succeed.

In the unequivocal state of the mind, intention is not a location or a position it is the state of the mind.

So many people think that they think. The mind is used to think reflect and reason. You will remain blind with your eye open until you can see with your mind by thinking.

There is no favoritism in accurate and precise calculation

Although knowledge is power, information is the key and gateway to a great future.

It will take the hand of God to move the hand of man.

With the backing of the great wise God, nothing will disconnect you from your inheritance.

As long as you have wisdom and understanding of God, Satan and evil cannot manipulate your life and destiny.

You have come this far by yourself judgment and decision you have made in the past, now lean and listen to God for another dimension of greatness.

Great people are common people it is extra ordinary effort and the price of sacrifice that produces greatness.

As a mental direct care worker I saw a great pastor and a motivational speaker within myself.

Menial job does not reduce your self-worth, until you resolve to achieve greatness see greatness in all you do; you will never count in your community

Chapter 2 - The Mind of Christ

The principle of Jesus will solve your gambling and addiction problems

The man of Jesus will lead you into heaven,

Everyone have their self-appraisal and what they think about you. Until you discover yourself other opinion about you will alter the real you.

Supervisors and directors are just a position in the chain of command in a work place. Never allow your supervisor hierarchy to alter your opinion about yourself.

Everyone can come out of debt if they make up their mind.

That I am not a decision maker at work does not diminish my contribution to my world.

Although it appears like it was a poor decision to accept a direct care employment at a psychiatric hospital as I reflect of my nine years of experience, it became apparent that I have learnt and experienced enough for my next assignment.

Self-encouragement and determination is a resolve of the heart.

If you are determined to make a difference, and do the things that make a difference you will eventually make a difference.

Good things do not come easy

Short cuts will cut your life short.

Those who look ahead move ahead.

Life is all about making an impact. In your life time strive to make an impact in your community.

Make friends and connect with people who are moving ahead of you in life.

If you can look around well you have come a long way in your life, made a lot of difference and realized a lot of success in life.

If you are my old friend, hurry up to reach out to me before I become a stranger to you.

Everything I am blessed with inspirations from God, that change my definition and interpretation of the world around me.

I thought I was stagnant and lonely until I looked around and noticed my children running around and my wife cooking.

Chapter 2 - The Mind of Christ

At 40 I resigned my Job to seek the Lord forever.

My ministry took a drastic rise to the top when the wisdom of God visited me with knowledge and understanding.

You will be a better person if you understand the characteristics of your personality – your mood swings attitudes and habits.

It is the seed of love you sow into the heart of a child and a woman that you reap in due time.

Love is not selfish, love share everything including the concealed secrets of the mind.

As long as you have a prayer life and a bible; you will never feel lonely, rejected and idle in the race of life.

When good friends disconnect from you, let them go, they might have seen something new in a different direction.

Confidence in yourself and in God is the only way to bring you out of captivity

Never train a child to waste his/her time.

The mind is the greatest assets of a great future.

You walk by common sense run by principles and fly by instruction.

Those who fly in flight of life fly alone.

Up in the air you are alone. No one can toll you accept the compass of knowledge and information

I have seen a tolling vehicle I have seen a tolling ship I have never seen a tolling airplane.

I exercise my judgment and make a decision every minute of the day.

Decisions are crucial, critical and vital with reference to your future.

So many people wish for a great future. You can only work towards a great future.

Your celebrity status began when you discovered your talent. What are you good at? Work at it with all commitment.

Prayers will sustain you but the wisdom of God will prosper you.

When I met Oyedepo, his teachings changed my perspective, but when I met Ibiyeomie; His teaching changed my perception.

I will be successful in ministry if only I concentrate and focus my energy in the work of the ministry.

It took the late Dr. Vincent Pearle Norman's book to open my mind towards kingdom success.

CHAPTER 3
PRAYER OF SALVATION

"Neither is there salvation in any other: for there is none other name under heaven given among men, whereby we must be saved." **Acts4:12.**

Salvation means deliverance from sin and the destruction of the forces of the devil. Are you saved?

What must I do to determine my salvation?

To be saved we must be born again! The word says as many as received him, to them gave He power to become the sons of God. Even to them that believe on his name.

To qualify for divine visitation do the following sincerely,

1) Acknowledge that you are a sinner and that He died for you. **Rom3:23.**

2) Repent of your sins. **Acts 3:19, Luke13:5, 2Peter3:9**

3) Believe in your heart that Jesus died for your sin. **Romans10:10**

4) Confess Jesus as the Lord over your life. **Romans10:10, Acts2:21**

Now repeat this Prayer after me

Say Lord Jesus, I accept you today, as my Lord and my savior, forgive me of my sins wash me with your blood. Right now, I believe, I am sanctified, I am save, I am free, I am free from the Power of sin to serve the Lord Jesus. Thank you Lord for saving me. Amen.

Congratulations:

YOU ARE NOW A BORN AGAIN CHRISTAIN

AGAIN I SAY TO YOU CONGRATULATION

I adjure you to watch the Spirit of God bear witness with your Spirit confirming His word with signs following.

Chapter 3 - Prayer of Salvation

The word says The Spirit itself beareth witness with our spirit, that we are the children of God.

MIRACLE CARE OUTREACH

"...But that the members should have the same care one for another" **1cor12:25**

We are all members of the body of Christ. Jesus commanded us to love our neighbor as ourselves. This includes caring for one another as a member of one body. True love is expressed in caring and giving. The word says for God so Love He gave….

Reach out to someone in need of Jesus, help someone in crisis find Christ. Look out and prove your love to Jesus by caring and inviting your friends and associates to find Jesus the Healer.

Invite your friends to our Home Care Cell Fellowship (Miracle chapel Intl Satellite fellowship) In the USA at 33 Schley Street Newark New Jersey 07112.

If you are in Nigeria—**MIRACLE OF GOD MINISTRIES**

A.K.A "MIRACLE CHAPEL INTL" Mpama –Egbu-Owerri Imo state Nigeria.

(Home Care Cell fellowship Group). We meet every Tuesday at 6:00pm-7:00pm.

LIFE IS NOT ALL ABOUT DURATION BUT ITS ALL ABOUT DONATION

What does the above statement mean?....

"Life consists not in accumulation of material wealth.." **Luke 12:15.**

"But it's all about liberality....meaning- what you can give and share with others." **Proverb 11:25.**

When you live for others--You live forever- because you out live your generation by the legacy you live behind after you depart into glory to be with the Lord.

Chapter 3 - Prayer of Salvation

But when you live to yourself - you are reduced to self—you are easily forgotten when you die and depart in glory.

Permit me to admonish you today to live your life to be a blessing to a soul connected to you today. I want you to know that so many souls are connected and looking up to you, and through you so many souls will be saved and rescued from destruction. Will you disciple someone today to find Jesus Christ?

"As a genuine Christian; it is your duty to evangelize Jesus Christ to all you meet on your way. Jesus is still in the healing business-Jesus is still doing miracles from time of old to now.

Therefore tell someone about Jesus Christ today, disciple and bring them to Church."

John 1:45 Philip findeth Nathanael....

Please to prove the sincerity of your love for God today; please become a soul winner. The dignity of your Christianity is hidden in your boldness to proclaim and evangelize Jesus Christ to all you meet on your way.

There is a question mark on the integrity of your Christianity until you become a life soul winner. Invite someone to join us worship the Lord Jesus this coming Sunday.

Amen

Chapter 3 - Prayer of Salvation

MIRACLE OF GOD MINISTRIES

PILLARS OF THE COMMISSION

We Believe Preach and Practice the following,

1) We believe and preach Salvation to every living human being

2) We believe and preach Repentance and forgiveness of sins

3) We believe and preach the baptism of the Holy Spirit and Spiritual gifts

4) We believe and teach the Prosperity

5) We believe and preach Divine Healing and Miracles (Signs &Wonder)

6) We believe and preach Faith

7) We believe and Proclaim the Power of God (Supernatural)

8) We believe and Proclaim Praise& Worship to God

9) We believe and preach Wisdom

10) We believe and preach Holiness (Consecration)

11) We believe and preach Vision

12) We believe and teach the Word of God

13) We believe and teach Success

14) We believe and practice Prayer

15) We believe and teach Deliverance

This 15 stones form the Pillars of Our Commission.

Become part of this church family and follow this great move of God.

MY HEART FELT PRAYER FOR YOU

It is always my prayer for you to give a new testimony. Every time I pray over your life, I expect a testimony from you.

Chapter 3 - Prayer of Salvation

Now let me Pray for you:

Lord Jesus, I give you thanks and praise this day. Father visit this precious one reading this book. Lord do that which no one can do for me. I thank you for saving me. I give you praise. I give thanks. In Jesus Mighty Name.

EXPECT A MIRACLE

If you are expecting a miracle write me back

Pastor Franklin N Abazie,
33 Schley street Newark,
New Jersey 07112

Or visit our ministry online

www.fnabaziehealingministries.org

I love for you to become an active member of this ministry. If you cannot join us physically, you can become part of us through your financial commitment. You can only attract what you respect. The way you treat a man of God will determine how God will reacts towards you.

Worship Center

MIRACLE OF GOD MINISTRIES
343 Sanford Avenue
Newark   New Jersey 07106

The Mind of Prayer

Prayer must become our custom and daily ritual for daily survival. Prayer means login into the mind of God to download divine intelligence to survive the devils wiles and schemes in life. The mind of Christ in my opinion is the mind of prayer. I encourage you to develop a mind of prayer. If you can pray enough you will prevail over your present circumstances.

Say this prayer out loud.

Say…. Father I give you thanks and praise today. I thank you for my life and for everything you have done in my life today. Lord Jesus transform my heart. Give me a spirit of love and worship. Lord do that which no man can do in life. I give you thanks and Praise, in Jesus Name. **AMEN.**

CHAPTER 4
ABOUT THE AUTHOR

Rev Franklin N Abazie is the founding and Presiding Pastor of Miracle of God Ministries with headquarters in Newark, New Jersey USA and a branch church in Owerri- Imo State Nigeria. He is following the footsteps of one of his mentors, Oral Roberts (Healing Evangelist) of the blessed memory.

The Lord passed Oral Roberts healing mantle two days before he went to be with the Lord at age 91 into the hand of healing evangelist-Rev Franklin N Abazie in a vision.

In all his services the Power and Presence of God is present to heal all in his audience. He is an ordained man of God with a Healing Ministry reviving the healing and miracle ministry of Jesus Christ of Nazareth.

Pastor Franklin N Abazie, is called by God with a unique mandate:

"THE MOMENT IS DUE TO IMPACT YOUR WORLD THROUGH THE REVIVAL OF THE HEALING & MIRACLE MINISTRY OF JESUS CHRIST OF NAZARETH.
I AM SENDING YOU TO RESTORE HEALTH UNTO THEE AND I WILL HEAL THEE OF THY WOUNDS. SAID THE LORD OF HOST"

He is a gifted ardent Teacher of the word of God who operates also in the office of a Prophet, generating and attracting undeniable signs & wonders, special miracles and healings, with apostolic fireworks of the Holy Ghost.

He is the founding and presiding senior Pastor of this fast growing Healing ministry.

Chapter 4 - About the Author

He has written over 86 inspirational, healing and transforming books covering almost all aspect of divine healing and life. He is happily married and blessed with children.

BOOKS BY REV FRANKLIN N ABAZIE

1) Commanding Abundance
2) The outcome of faith
3) Understanding the secret of prevailing prayers
4) Understanding the secret of the man God uses
5) Activating my due Season
6) Overcoming Divine Verdicts
7) The Outcome of Divine Wisdom
8) Understanding God's Restoration Mandate
9) Walking in the Victory and Authority of the truth
10) Gods Covenant Exemption
11) Destiny Restoration Pillars
12) Provoking Acceptable Praise
13) Understanding Divine Judgment
14) Activating Angelic Re-enforcement
15) Provoking Un-Merited Favor
16) The Benefits of the Speaking faith
17) Understanding Divine Arrangement

18) Understanding Divine Healing
19) The Mystery of Endurance
20) Obeying Divine Instructions
21) Understanding the Voice of God
22) Never give up on Hope
23) The prevailing Power of faith
24) Understanding Divine Prosperity
25) The Reward of Prayer
26) Covenant Keys to Answered Prayers
27) Activating the Forces of Vengeance
28) Put your faith to work
29) Where is your trust?
30) The Audacity of the Blood of Jesus
31) Redeeming Your Days
32) The force of Vision
33) Breaking the shackles of Family Curses
34) Wisdom for Marriage Stability
35) The winners Faith
36) The Prayer solution
37) The power of Prayer
38) Prayer strategy
39) The prayer that works
40) Walking in Forgiveness
41) The power of the grace of God

42) The power of Persistence
43) Overcoming Divine verdicts
44) The audacity of the blood of Jesus.
45) The prevailing power of the blood of Jesus
46) The benefit of the speaking faith.
47) Fearless faith
48) Redeeming Your Days.
49) The Supernatural Power of Prophecy
50) The companionship of the Holy Spirit
51) Understanding Divine Judgement
52) Understanding Divine Prosperity
53) Dominating Controlling Forces
54) The winners Faith
55) Destiny Restoration Pillars
56) Developing Spiritual Muscles
57) Inexplicable faith
58) The lifestyle of Prayer
59) Developing a positive attitude in life.
60) The mystery of Divine supply
61) Encounter with God's Power
62) Walking in love
63) Praying in the Spirit
64) How to provoke your testimony

65) Walking in the reality of the Anointing
66) The reality of new birth
67) The price of freedom
68) The Supernatural power of faith
69) The Power of Persistence
70) The intellectual components of Redemption
71) Overcoming Fear
72) The Force of Vision
73) Overcoming Prevailing Challenges
74) The Power of the Grace of God
75) My life & Ministry
76) The Mystery of Praise

MIRACLE OF GOD MINISTRIES

NIGERIA CRUSADE 2012

MIRACLE OF GOD MINISTRIES
NIGERIA CRUSADE 2012

MIRACLE OF GOD MINISTRIES

NIGERIA CRUSADE

2012

MIRACLE OF GOD MINISTRIES

NIGERIA CRUSADE

2012

www.ingramcontent.com/pod-product-compliance
Lightning Source LLC
Chambersburg PA
CBHW021448080526
44588CB00009B/741